IRRATIONAL ME

NISHA M. S.

To GuruParampara

Contents

Acknowledgements

Thank you collective intelligence of universe, Guru Parampara, Rishi Parampara, holy sidhas, seers, sages, saints, prophets, archangels, archetypes, preceptors, spiritual masters, all Gurus of KrishnaMani, KrishnaMani ma'am, all the teachers for making me able to do this.

Thank you, Kiran, for planting the idea of publishing in me.

KrishnaMani and all my soul family members, you are the energy that is formed as the words inside this book.

Thankyou Amma, Achan, Nidhin and Devika for all the love and support.

Thank you Sherin sir for being the reason of this content.

Thank you, all my friends, for always trusting in me.

1

Chapter 1

Learning is a continuous and an inevitable process in everyone's life. It is the process of learning that makes each individual unique and different. A child begins to learn from the moment of birth. Learning can be exciting in many ways. But the same time it can be the most challenging thing happened to you in your entire life.

I had an eventful childhood and my academic learning was very smooth and a happy experience in childhood. My mother was a primary school teacher and she taught me how to read and write in very early age. So, by the time I started schooling I was already in track of exploring books. My father is also an inspiration for my reading. He stills reads multiple newspapers and other periodicals on a daily basis. He had a decent collection of books which mostly discussed communist ideology. Even though he is a passionate person who is followed his ideology up to this day, he never wanted to make a biased concept in me about any ideology or in any other topics. I now believe that he denied my reading from his collection for creating a new and my own perspective about everything.

But as a child my curiosity was that he might have some interesting stories in his collection which he do not wish to share with me. But my mom was providing me with numerous children's literature books from her school library to satiate my hunger for reading. I have read almost everything in my school library by the time of 4th standard.

When someone says not to do a particular thing, its natural to have an increased curiosity and you can imagine why I sneak into his my dad's collection multiple times. So he introduced me to our local library with strict guidelines to the librarian that only children's books were allowed me to access.

I agree it was fun to read about stories where animals talk and using magic. I almost believed that magic can be possible and its just I cant experience it and I wanted to believe that animals, plants and other inanimate objects can talk just like us. Pots, pipes, pillows and a lot of other house hold items thus had space in my childhood play times because every item was able to talk to me. Or as I now say, I was an excellent dialogue creator who spoke for every character in play times.

With the excuse of finishing up all the available children's literature in library I gradually moved to Malayalam literature and for long-time classic Malayalam novels were the love of my life. I even had a pattern of finishing up all the works by an author before moving to the next author.

I never filtered my reading lists for fiction or fantasy. I loved reading anything that can take me to a world of imagination. Stories always had a lot of details that allowed me to imagine for a very long time. when it is pure fantasy I could think about if it was rail and if it had happened to me. Most stories that talked about the time before me, it was a timeline travel.

I laughed, wept, smiled, aroused, excited, felt bad, travelled through a lot of lands, met a lot of people, listened to their thoughts and feelings and simply experienced everything that can be experienced through literature. This reading itself made up most of my childhood.

Next phase of my reading was translation literature. By this time, I had finished my high school and had found access to bigger library with where librarian treated me like an adult reader. With my limited access in my local library I was struggling to find new and exciting stuff to read. One of my school extra-curricular activity was a literature festival held in an yearly manner. My teachers put me up for a literature review competition where I had to write reviews of around 50 books and submit on the festival day. Even though I was very good at reading speed I never treated my reading as part of my education. It was a fun activity like playing where I don't have to keep track of whatever I read. So my submission was very bad in quantity. I couldn't even remember 50 book names, so how about writing about them. I casually submitted a couple of reviews and happily wandered around the school ground on the festival day. School competitions had a pattern which I was so familiar with. We gather, participate, return. If you had won, somehow your teachers will know. You can go and collect your prize at a designated time and venue. If you didn't win the last part simply doesn't happen. As a participant I was always in the comfort zone. I was happy if I win something, but I was totally cool about not winning too. Something my mom taught me so thoroughly, she hated the drama of not winning something, which was very common on any competition event.

But in this literature festival, I was mistaken. During the evaluation phase, our team of participants hangs out freely. There will be no pressure of performing anything so it was actually the fun part of any event. We had a set of students who repeatedly appeared for most of the events so we were able to have a relationship with a lot of non-classmates. Some of my best friends are from these relationships and hang outs. So during hangout time, I was called to report at the evaluation spot. I met an active library council member who was holding my submission. He questioned me about the lack of quantity. I was frightened because I never expected that. I was never hoping to win but also never anticipated any further consequences. So I was startled by this intervention. But his real intention was giving me access to better source for my reading. Somehow he was impressed with my minimal quantity review submission and he welcomed me to take a library membership at their library.

I was so excited to have access to more books and continued to read novels for a while but after a while he encouraged me to try translated literature. That was next phase of my learning where I came to know a lot of new and exciting things. Unknown countries with unknown cultures, traditions, language, religion and cuisine, I was in for a free imaginary world tour. In all stories despite of all their differences I was able to find happiness. Because whatever the feeling a book can provide, upon finishing I was able to take a deep breath and enjoy the closure of each reading journey and savor it for the coming few days. Sometimes I may be haunted by the characters and emotions in the story. But I was happy about that. And after the literature festival incident I kept track of everything I read.

The experience brought by the translation literature was entirely different from what I experienced in all those previous years. Reading became an effortful task because when it get translated, lot of sentences turns to complicated units of expression. During my college years, I have high lightened and underlined more pages and lines in Orhan Pamuk's works than my engineering textbooks. Let me say it was never my intention to become the ir(rational) me when I started learning engineering.

Engineering was all about logic and rational thinking. My discipline was computer science and very soon I hated coding. It was all fitting in strict frameworks. Syntaxes, algorithms, mathematics all made me feel bored all day. My bright academic record hit a big block there with abundance of failed papers. I don't remember a lot of things from there. But I can still sense my feeling regarding computer labs. Whenever I pull back the chair in computer lab, I feel like I am going to interact with a dead thing which act like alive only because of electricity. It was a very cold experience and I hated air conditioning too.

So I began to immerse myself in the limited literature collection in our technical library and began to carry books from my home town to campus. My reading was getting more serious than ever. By that time I had gained the non positive image from majority of faculties. But teachers can always amuse us. So for me too it was my tutor from engineering college who turned the page of my life into the bright light of irrational world. He was not happy with the direction of my academic life and even if he doesn't have to, he intervened with my life. He pushed me to practice a better lifestyle and my parents and friends were always there to support me.

It began as a simple yoga course in my hometown. A few months of practice, my thoughts began to flow in different direction. My yoga trainer once told me that there is an entirely unknown world out here that I can not sense with my sensory systems.

It struck me so hard that for a while I paused literature reading and start exploring ancient Indian scriptures. I never dropped literature. But it was reaching the optimum. So in search of the unknown world I choose psychology and started learning again. I never went back to my first college to clear the failed papers. Psychology was rich and powerful enough to satiate my reading hunger in the most exciting way. I am talking a lot about my reading because it is an integral part of the ir(rational) me.

2

Chapter 2

Psychology learning was a life changing event in my life. Initially the syllabus was flooded with different sort of contents. We had to study different papers on language, statistics, and physiology and even history. So, among these other subjects we had relatively low psychology learning. Most of psychology graduate students may have come across this doubt that, "I actually enrolled for psychology not this". But with my age difference from other students, I was more patient. I waited for full day long, travelled kilometers on a daily basis just for a few moments of psychology learning. It was worthy. I had brilliant teachers who as bale to lay strong foundation of subject as well as lasting passion on the discipline.

But the process of learning was happening in a slow but steady rate. Understanding the basic concepts really requires time. On initial reading we get certain level of learning, but deeper understanding happens in course of time.

Psychology has numerous interesting branches. So it is actually difficult to chose one from. During undergraduate psychology course, I was just getting familiarized with all the aspects. I was unsure about a lot of things. But the learning was always fun and exciting.

The result of learning or actual change was in my personality. For me the troublemaker student in engineering college turned into a very satisfactory student, the problematic friend in me turned into a person with healthy relationships, the rebel daughter became understanding person and within the few years all of my old friends, and family started to testify that Nisha have changed.

Under graduate years was molding me into a person who always check for the other person's perspective. When you are in a crowded bus and co passengers are pushing you, I was able to think that they are pushing me just for them to breathe or balance not to hurt me. When a sales person treats me impolitely, I was able to think that he/she may be burnt out. I was not perfect in regulating my emotions but I was able to understand them.

I was a chatty person back in engineering college. As a psychology student I was learning to listen. It was not easy. But we learned. Everyone was trying to be better listeners. Learning skills was more important than memorizing theories. We had our moments in campus life but somehow everyone was able to learn something in perspective of behavioral science from every incidents.

3

Chapter 3

Human mind is designed to seek answers. I usually found it quite satisfactory to get an accurate answer whenever I seek some questions. An Answer is actually a closure. life is mostly uncertain and sometimes closures make us feel certain again. When you learn any discipline in depth certain questions comes to us like the challenging block in games that never lets us to the next stage or level. I found it very difficult to create answers with the existing knowledge. It was a constant feeling that I need something more, or something is still out there which my curriculum can not provide me. Psychology can be defined using a number of definitions. Ancient definitions mentioned its intention to learn soul. By the time I started learning, it has grown a lot and was focusing on human behavior. Today the discipline is better represented by the term behavioral science.

My yoga trainer's mentioning about another parallel world was upsetting me. I had a gut feeling that it might be true. Or I wanted it to be true and I was in search of it even if I was not sure about the existence. I had a lot of time to spare during undergraduate studies. So I started exploring other sources to gain more information.

When it comes to the founding questions of human existence, or who am I type questions, internet is not that appealing. Or I was unable to find adequate answers in it. This ascension of search is universal. Maslow has dictated this beautifully through his need hierarchy.

It says what a person needs in his life through out the journey. Preliminary needs of a human being is food. This is the existential need when one is struggling to meet their living. Times has been changed and food or water may not be the primary need of every person. But it implies that an organism's primary need is the means for physical survival. The aids can be different according to the situations. It can be food, water or the basic earning for a living. When people meet this need, they had to search for a higher need. It is the safety needs. To be in a safe place is the need of everyone. After meeting the safety measures, one begins to seek for love. This is the social part. Humans are social animal and hence they will search for the social acceptance part. Having friends and a social life comes under this perspective. Then comes the higher needs like need for self-esteem and ultimate path to self-actualization. Physical needs and safety needs might be present all the times because it is part of existence. I have met some difficulties with meeting these existential needs but they were never permanent. So it was natural to grow into higher needs by time. it was all coming in synchrony with my psychology learning. Soon I started learning it, these questions has been visiting me now and then. With the excitement of new discipline I ignored these questions for a while. I learned the Maslow's hierarchy in my UG class. So when you confront the questions right inside the discipline, its hard to avoid them. I was forced to search answers not to become a hypocrite.

Just like the academic system in India, which is bachelors, masters and then to master and doctor of philosophy, I too leaned to philosophy. Being an Indian citizen, the most easily accessible philosophy was Indian. (there were so many compelling choices out there). Most Indian scriptures discuss a secret nature of delivering wisdom through a master (Guru). I was so intrigued by the idea of having a Guru. When I finally arrived at the answer that all my answers lies at Guru I was relieved. Because it was just a matter of finding a Guru. Then I will be at the verge of every answers. My life is going to be complete.

The thought train itself generate a doubt. Is that simple as that? I learned it the hard way. It is never easy. Finding your Guru is possible only by grace of Guru.

Inability to find answers inside the science textbooks was the first step of being ir(rational) me. It was easy for me to go for some job after college. I may not be the best coder, I was sure I could find some job out there and start my career. Instead I believed in a discipline to give me answers to the questions of life and within very short time I was convinced that it is not that easy.

Finding a Guru or even accepting the fact that my questions will be answered only through a Guru was hit to my rational self. All the readings I ever had including the sneaky readings of communist ideology raised before me like a giant monster.

I had to to try the irrational option to know whether it is true or not. So with the doubt in mind I searched for a Guru. Back in the time of Yoga training, I had met some people who already had a Guru and thus I was familiar with the settings. But it is not like search something in Google and going right to the website with answers. That is where the secret nature comes bashing in our face. Even if we are wanting it so much it was difficult to find. I didn't know the means to search, I didn't know if I really wanted to search and I was particularly unsure about what happens after the search.

Since I was trained as a science student, I had to test. Only after testing you can decide the answer. Science is always about experimenting. So I conveniently include my trial for irrational me inside the the experimental part and thus fulfilled the criteria of rational me.

I was seeing a lot of coincidences at this time. everything was leading me toward a Guru. My lifestyle was gradually changing. I began to avoid non vegetarian food. My stomach was getting upset when I eat meat. I was getting intolerant to smell of fish and eggs were too difficult for my sinuses. But I loved junk foods. I drank a lot of carbonated drinks, was fond of processed food and spicy foods were my favorite. But my body continuously showed me signs saying it doesn't want all that. At the beginning it was easy to ignore symptoms and proceed with cravings. But gradually it became more difficult to avoid them.

Practicing yoga asanas became more fun. I found happiness in doing yoga, sitting and chanting etc.

When you are inside the psychology discipline the most annoying thing is the presence of false people. People who claim of having scientific knowledge, people who are intentionally manipulating the scientific knowledge, people who believe in the pseudo science and disputes within the scientifically trained people.

Nobody knows the intensity and depth of conflicts inside the discipline unless you become the part of it. This is in addition to the struggles one has to face as a person. For me it was the bad academic history from college, pressure to get married and seeing all my friends getting settled into luxury lives just like we were all meant to be.

I constantly compared myself to my friends, knowing how much they earn, how dependent am I on my parents, why should I marry someone to all this uncertainties, how can I deal my family if I didn't get married and so on. So inside the rational self of seeking right answers, I always wished for some magic to happen and turn my life around.

It was easy to think like that. Just with a wave of a magic wand everything getting settled. So easy..

That is why when I got an opportunity to reach to a master I took it without hesitating. Part of me was wishing for it for a while and finally I met her.

4

Chapter 4

When you begin your search for meaning of life, a lot of options comes to you. World welcomes you with a lot of choices. Philosophical, religious and spiritual interpretations methods and a lot more comes to you like a shopping app. If you are a selective shopper, you have to take a tremendous effort to choose one. If you are selective and same time rational, there will be additional time requirements. But this selection process does not actually provides that much choices as it seems. Unless you don't chose a single path it is most impossible to find the meaning in search. It is simple process. You have to choose a product in order to buy it. Similarly you have to choose one path in order to find the answer.

Sometimes you drop the shopping process itself because of the difficulties with the choice. You can survive without having that particular product, but it is not the as same as having it. Deep down in your mind, it will haunt you sometimes.

After carefully choosing and even after having the feeling of satisfaction at the moment of choosing, the recurrent thought of "was it right" starts to tickle you once in a while.

Choosing one school of thought and analyzing entire life based on that thought school is a hectic task. Since all this happens inside your brain, millions of data bits are ready to interfere your analysis at any point.

We say we own our thoughts. But the concept of homunculus is a contradictory thing. I have always felt something similar to homunculus from very young times. Now for a fact I am certain that it was no hallucination. Rather it is a sense that someone is a talking to you rationally as well as irrationally at many occasions and it is a form of self-talk. But believing the presence of a second person there, was kind of interesting and fun for me.

So I was somewhat prepared when I reached my Guru. Learning was rapid and changes were clearly visible. The challenge was when it came to irrational thinking. One saying I often found conflicting was when my Guru asks to practice Prathipaksha bhavana or opposition thinking. It is the process of thinking exactly opposite to what is existing. When you really don't have a solution to some problems, I was asked to say that there is solution. How is it right, many of us asked often. The answer was simply, you have to think what actually you want and what you actually see.

For any person with a normal life apart from the spiritual practicing, this seemed almost impossible. When you have so much anger towards someone, how can you chant that I love that person. But out of respect and love toward Guru we practiced it.

The learning I got from there was always resulted in good experiences. Personal changes were the most beautiful. I felt a lot of peace. I was happy all the times. Whenever this peacefulness, or happiness changed, we had the training to face it and tools to change it.

I was in search of a lot answers and I revived a lot of them from there. But the practice took times. One other practice I learned was to observe my thoughts and correct them whenever it is not positive. Now, when I wrote it, it finished in just a sentence. In reality I took years to practice that. Most of the time some thoughts will be wandering through our brain, but we never realizes them. At least I never realized my own thoughts before. When I started to observe them I could see all the explanations of my own behavior. Introspection has been read and learned through textbooks. But doing it was a novel experience.

Observing is one thing, changing them to positive ones was the other task. But when you realize how much non positive things are streaming through your neurons, a tendency to make changes is natural. Replacing all non positive words was fun and exciting. I learned a lot of new words to replace the ones I used to say. I could say non positive instead of the term negative.

Bringing your continuous attention to thoughts is a mindful process. You can not do things mechanically when you are observing yourself. Writing affirmations, saying chants and a lot of other practices was in my learning. I was trying all these alongside of psychology learning.

Both these learning were in the beginning phase and it was both exciting so I never had to be concerned during these initial phase.

5

Chapter 5

When I was about to apply for post-graduation, I just had a few criteria. A place near to my home, a nice campus, and a good library. My campus was fitting in all of my requirements. I sent out only one application. My teachers were so upset with me for making no other choice. They asked me the logical question of what if it didn't come through. I somehow was didn't made any other choices. I was not absolutely sure about my admission. Hundreds of candidates were applying for couple of seats. Being in the top five was a bare necessity for admission and I made it.

But I was practicing my other learning at the same time. I was trained to accept whatever I receive. So getting admission and not getting admission had to be dealt with an acceptance. I repeatedly thought about getting in, wrote affirmations, literally wrote gratitude for my previous educations, I wrote thanks to all my teachers from nursery to college and I studied.

I was trained to see the end result only, so I trusted the process and keep visualising the end result which is getting admission.

Campus was a beautiful place to live. It was so inexpensive to live. We didn't have to pay a lot of fees but had the best facilities for learning. Here, focus was different psychology papers. So I was able to focus on psychology. Campus was always active. Living in campus always felt good. Our faculties were always available, so we had great relationship.

At post graduation, there were more of a discussion based learning than lecturing. Our batch was just ten girls. It was more of round sitting arrangement and open discussions most times. We were all passionate about psychology but everyone had their doubts in making it into a profession. To start practice, we all needed a lot of pushing from our teachers. Knowing it is one thing, applying it into helping one in need is complex. Individual differences are always present, so each person has to be managed in a new and unique way. Generalisations are overrated in therapy. We had great training from the university. Our fellow students from other disciplines cooperated a lot. They were willing to consult us even if we were in learning phase.

Post-graduation also focused on research. i learned research methodology and had to conduct many researches as part of the programme. Each research irrespective of its size was important. Research findings are one of the many results of a research. Major result is the change happening inside the researcher. The process was always challenging but I had to and I did it with great pleasure.

Here comes the rational part. A scientific research is the systematic method to reach at the answer of a research question. It has different steps. Defining the problem, formulating a hypothesis, testing the hypothesis, reaching at the answer and then documenting it. We ere taught to see everything with a suspicion in order to find the truth through the methods of science. When it comes to study behaviour, the discipline itself has not yet reached all goals of science. Science always describe, explain, predict and control a phenomenon. Behaviour can be described, explained mostly, predicated to some extent and controlled moderately.

This is something discussed in the very beginning of research methodology. So sometimes it feels like we have lot to grow before meeting the goals. Neuroscience is the best area that has been able to provide scientific background to psychology. It rely on scientific methods to study behaviour. In neuro scientific perspective, thoughts can be detected as electrical signals and using technology a lot of explanations are possible. Learning about brain was fun. I was fascinated by many facts about what happens in brain when you do something. How neural connections are made, how they are faded, how similar our brain is to a computer and a lot more. Our university was based on Sree Sankaracharya and hence we had to learn Indian philosophy, I was already interested in it and the learning was easy. We practiced Yoga too.

Consistent practicing of different limbs of Yoga makes a lot of changes inside and out. Mindfulness was part of daily practice. It started from cafeteria where I invested a lot of time to savour each bite of food. I was always observing, experimenting and learning through the method of science. Critical thinking and questioning was daily practice.

After that when I turn to my spiritual side, I had to do a lot of irrational things like saying affirmation, writing gratitude and most importantly releasing my non positive emotions without lag. Catharsis is not a new concept, but doing it whenever you feel a non-pleasant feeling was not common. Through physical exercises and deep breaths I vented my non positive feelings. I was doing this only because I felt good about that. I found no explanations for this.

I was beginning to question myself. When I follow a path of scientific research how am I supposed to follow a lifestyle where being rational is not fitting. I kept on thinking. When I read scriptures all I could think was am I doing some foolish things. Then I will come back to the thought that I am just experimenting.

It was the beginning of my inner conflict. Who am I? rational or irrational?

Then a family member passed away. Usually when someone close to us pass away, we go through a grieving process. The beginning stages are usually hard an lot of emotional expressions are the stereotype.

It was nothing like the stereotype within my spiritual family. All of them faced the situation with a lot of balance and acceptance. They were able to talk about it, accept the situation and look for solutions. Everyone was there to support each other.

I was struggling to understand this behaviour. I was okay to be irrational about a lot of things. But when it came to intense emotions, I was not ready to be irrational. It was my choice. Nobody challenged me about my choice.

Around this time, I had a personal talk with one of my teachers and he mentioned his knowledge about my spiritual whereabouts. That was a long conversation where I listened his concerns about how I was being irrational about those practices when actually I am in a field of rational thinking.

From the childhood it was my nature to carry on thoughts for days. I kept thinking about it over and over. I was getting confused, getting emotional and I couldn't think effectively. Thought process was overwhelmed by the conflicts and emotions.

The life I chose outside my profession was turning into an unpleasant feeling.

6

Chapter 6

I was the only responsible person for all my decisions. I couldn't deal with the dilemma. So I distracted myself with academics. I spent a lot of time reading, writing and hanging out with friends and family completely avoiding any spiritual practices.

Each time when a habit gets invoked like chanting or saying affirmation, I talked to myself, it is not rational. You are not supposed to. And I suddenly stopped. Now I feel this as the second phase of my experimentation.

I was seeing people only in my academic circle and before them I could be my best. But whenever I do something amazing and receive a compliment, I realised the reflection of my spiritual learning in that.

I felt guilty for not practicing it anymore and yet receiving the benefits. In many instances it was possible for me to break a lot of learning. But I didn't wanted to. And it felt so good to keep all the good parts of learning. Now I can relate that everything was good about the spiritual learning.

Looking it all in an outsider and rational perspective was refreshing. I could see the changes that were brought up in me through the practices. But most of them were result of irrational practices. How can I feel good about the effects and not accept the cause?

Questions were always flooding to me. I avoided confrontations with myself and completely immersed into physical world. It was not fun. Everyday excitement was not there. When I do something, it felt mechanical. I was not happy as before. But the weirdest thing was I felt okay to struggle and suffer.

I don't consider such feeling as part of good mental health. When you are struggling, you should be able to realise and try to come out of it. But I never felt like doing anything about that.

If someone analysed me at that time, they may evaluate that I was doing okay. But I was doing better than that with my irrational self. It is impossible to show evidence for these two states of wellbeing. Rational world is all about evidence and irrational world has nothing but the experience. People who follow spiritual practices usually have to go through rituals and learning leaving all the doubts. Any doubt about the cause or effect can affect the process of learning. People who have such levels of submissions to a practice are the followers of that system.

7

Chapter 7

At many points you will get confused. Sensation and perception burst out from textbook definition and you start to observe and questioned the very own neurons in your brain. As I can't see what actually happened inside those cells the results of the cellular actions become questionable. Sometimes the perceptions indicate that those cells have nothing to do with what actually happens. It is a form of ecstasy. You will no longer feel any sort of sadness. Even the life around you try to make you feel pain you won't. By that time, I began to realize that pain and pleasure both are like illusions. if you look one more time at the cause of both pain and pleasure you will start to feel them differently. Then they are not anymore, those feelings. Rather it is something you haven't read anywhere in your textbook. I think out of body experience is a suitable term. The only connection you feel with the body is that some sort of string. Like I am actually a kite and is attached with this body with an infinite string. It's possible to fly as much distance as I want but there is always a light force in string that reminds me of that bodily connection.

Everyone at some point in their life which start looking for answers. That Quest has been described by many but once you start getting answers actually there are not many explanations about what to do while you receive those answers. Maybe the first one or two answers will feel okay. It was the end of a quest and I got a feeling of something achieved. But the flow of answers is infinite. Moment by moment you will get revelations, evidences real-time interactions, and unexplainable experiences. Slowly the initial sense of achievement turns into amusement, anxiety and then into a stillness. Now receiving answers is a habit. Even if there are no answers at the moment stillness is the same. The concept of time is a joke now. Whatever I learnt in Science textbooks about time is not accurate according to my perception. Yes, the clock ticks Earth rotates Seasons change but is that time? Or is it just a sequence and time is something else. Even the calculations, time is infinite and we don't know what infinite is. All of these aspects of rational thinking has some elements of unknown. Science starts from the big bang theory and is till searching for answers about universe.

For the sake of argument one can say that seeking answer with the aid of mathematics is accurate and right where attempting a similar task through irrational practices is not acceptable an wrong.

I am not sure about this too. But there are moments that makes us revisit this question and, in those moments, ir(rational) me happens.

At the end of day everyone wants peace and happiness. I have attended an online course named " Science of wellbeing" by a Yale professor. She teaches many practices that can make us happier and sustain that happiness. Some of those practices are writing gratitude and savouring the moments. Evidence suggest that expressing gratitude can have positive impact on your life. Spirituality teaches it as a way of living.

Conflict I had in my PG time affected me in depth and it took a flood to come back to the spiritual path. I was not terrified for my life. But everything we owned was about to lose, and we lost many things. In the mouth of danger it is hard to go for rational thinking. Or I was unable to. On the second day of flood, I started chanting again.

Maybe it is a set of sounds repeated to bore the brain, but it could bring peace to me in the crisis situations. At the moment of intense suffering, I only wanted a solution, not the explanation.

I was not going to be happy about the possible answer to the question of why this happened to me. I have asked that question a lot. I had some traumatic experiences in childhood and so I am an expert in asking that question. With the history of questioning over a decade, I learned that asking the question again and again is not contributing to my mental health. Leaving the unanswered questions and moving on is sometimes essential. But it takes a lot of effort and courage to move on.

With the passage of time, we may forget things. Human memory is able to repress unpleasant information. Usually it takes long and during the time people suffer in many ways. Spirituality treats all those unpleasant experiences as part of cycle of Karma. Concept of Karma and past lives are totally irrational. But it makes people reach at closure and gain acceptance.

Science intends to make the human life easier and happier. Irrational spirituality does the same.

So after the dilemma and flood I came back to the same campus for my research degree(MPhil). It was just an year and I tried the dual practice there. My close friends were amused as well as a little concerned by my methods. I never mixed up my practices with those concerned friends. It was in their and my best interest I separated these.

With a little bit of practice, I became able to think as a scientific researcher whenever I face a research question or while I am teaching or consulting. But in the personal life, I find it comforting to follow spiritual practices. It is my choice of living.

It may or may not be true to think that I get research ideas by the help of divine beings, or I am being protected by angels while I drive. I can assure that no harm is done by this synchronous rationality and irrationality in the same person. May be the human brains have evolved to handle two different thought streams inside a single organ.

Learning makes human different from other animals as well as among humans. Among a group of humans, the best learner thrives. Becoming the best learner is tough. So why not adopt multiple methods to attain maximum learning. It is possible to learn, unlearn and relearn. This ability makes the learning process exciting for eternity.

8

Chapter 8

It is time I conclude all my irrational and rational self. It was debate with myself. I just reported it for myself as part of learning. World is a dynamic place. Nothing remains the same here always. So the chances are leaning towards change and it is unpredictable. It is important to feel good about what you do. World is merely a reflection of our self. If you are happy you will perceive the world as a happy place. If you are not happy you may perceive the same as not a good place. Humans have a default tendency to focus on negative as part of our existential instincts. So it is probable to focus on non-positive things and getting sad.

Bringing something to attention is inevitable, but there is a choice in how long you want to manage it. In my practice, I focus more on positive things and spends very little on non positive aspects. I train people to express their feelings in healthy ways and then to take choice, whether to remain there or to move on.

Happiness only comes where there is a willingness to adapt, and adaption is the ultimate product of learning.

I irrationally say positive affirmations, do service(seva) to Guru Parampara, spend my earnings as per scriptural learning, follow rituals with thorough understanding and all of these are flexible practices. With the rational mind I address academic questions, do teach and provide therapy and training sessions. I never asks my clients to practice spirituality. But I do recommend practices like gratitude journaling accompanied by research evidences.

Spirituality and science both are derived by humans. Being irrational is fun for me, so I do that. Being rational is my job as a researcher, teacher and a psychologist, so I do that.

This is the ir(rationa)l me.

9 798886 294897

Printed by Libri Plureos GmbH in Hamburg,
Germany